I didn't know that some trains run on water

© Aladdin Books Ltd 1997
© U.S. text 1997
Produced by
Aladdin Books Ltd
28 Percy Street
London W1P 0LD

First published in the United States in 1997 by
Copper Beech Books,
an imprint of
The Millbrook Press
2 Old New Milford Road
Brookfield, Connecticut 06804

Concept, editorial, and design by
David West Children's Books

Illustrators: Ross Walton and Jo Moore

Printed in Belgium

Library of Congress Cataloging-in-Publication Data
Petty, Kate.
Some trains run on water : and other amazing facts about rail transportation /
Kate Petty ; illustrated by Ross Walton, Jo Moore.
p. cm. — (I didn't know that—)
Includes index.
Summary: Provides information about different types of trains,
including steam locomotives, electric trains, trams, and modern high-speed trains.
ISBN 0-7613-0598-X (HC.). — ISBN 0-7613-0609-9 (lib. bdg.)
1. Railroads—Juvenile literature. [1. Railroads.]
I. Walton, Ross, ill. II. Moore, Jo, ill. III. Title IV. Series.
TF148.P43 1997
625.1 — dc21
97-8236
CIP AC

I didn't know that

some trains run on water

Kate Petty

COPPER BEECH BOOKS
BROOKFIELD, CONNECTICUT

I didn't know that

Introduction

Did *you* know that trains opened up the American West? ... that the *Flying Hamburger* was a train?... that they can go upside down?

Discover for yourself amazing facts about rail transportation, from the earliest steam trains that traveled at walking pace to the latest technology of the high-speed supertrains.

 Watch for this symbol that means there is a fun project for you to try.

 Is it true or is it false? Watch for this symbol and try to answer the question before reading on for the answer.

Don't forget to check the borders for extra amazing facts.

I didn't know that

the first steam trains went slower than walking pace.

In 1804, Richard Trevithick's steam engine pulled ten tons of iron ore and 70 passengers over nine miles. It took four hours and five minutes. Trevithick walked ahead all the way.

SEARCH & FIND Can you find the running boy? FIND & SEARCH

In 1829, *Rocket,* built by George Stephenson, won a competition for the best steam engine. It had an average speed of 12 mph and a top speed of 29 mph.

Catch Me Who Can gave rides to fare-paying passengers.

! *Locomotion* was the first successful steam freight train.

True or false?
Horses pulled the first railroad trains for passengers.

Answer: **True**
Nearly 200 years ago passengers were pulled by horses on the world's first passenger line in Wales. The Emperor and Empress of Austria used this form of transportation 25 years later (above left).

I didn't know that

steam trains run on water.

A steam engine uses water to get its power. A coal fire heats the water. The boiling water turns to steam. The steam is forced into the *cylinders* where *pistons* are pushed that turn the wheels.

SEARCH & FIND
FIND & SEARCH

Follow the blue arrows to find where the water goes.

Boiler

Smokestack

Drive wheels

Pistons inside cylinder

Blast pipes

HIAWATHA
Steam locomotive

Trains can't always carry enough fuel
so on long journeys they have to
stop to take on more fuel
and water.

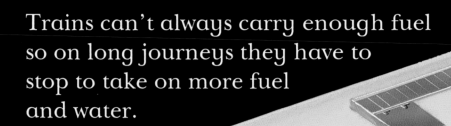

Tender

Water

Coal

Driver

Firebox

Fireman

As well as the driver who controls the
speed, reads the signals, and stops and
starts the train, each locomotive needs a
fireman to tend the boiler. It is his job to
stoke up the fire in the firebox and to
keep the boiler well supplied with water.

Railroads come in many different widths, or *gauges*.

I didn't know that

steam trains opened up the American West. By 1850, the railroad companies had bought the land and laid track from coast to coast. At last goods could get from factories in the East to the new towns in the West.

Sparks from the fire cool down in the smokestack, keeping them safe.

SEARCH & FIND & FIND & SEARCH &
Can you find the three train robbers?

Before steam trains, settlers traveled in wagon trains.

Two teams built the Union Pacific Railroad across America, starting from opposite ends. They met in Utah in 1869.

True or false?

Casey Jones was a famous train robber.

Answer: **False**

The real Casey Jones was an engineer who died in 1900 when his engine, the *Cannonball Express*, hit a freight train that was stalled. Casey knew he couldn't slow down fast enough. He made his fireman jump to safety, and all the passengers survived.

Early railroad travelers were often attacked by robbers or native Indians.

AMERICAN TYPE 4–4–0
Steam locomotive

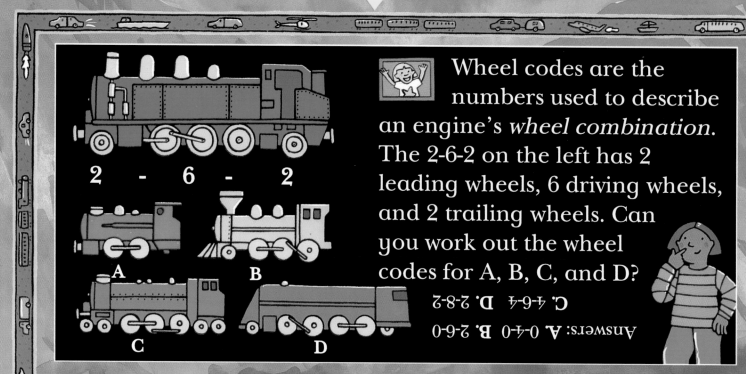

2 - 6 - 2

A

B

C

D

Wheel codes are the numbers used to describe an engine's *wheel combination.* The 2-6-2 on the left has 2 leading wheels, 6 driving wheels, and 2 trailing wheels. Can you work out the wheel codes for A, B, C, and D?

Answers: A. 0-4-0 B. 2-6-0 C. 4-6-4 D. 2-8-2

Mallard was a famous streamlined British steam engine. It set the steam speed record of 125 mph in 1938. This record has never been broken since!

One of the longest trains ever pulled 500 cars of coal.

I didn't know that

the biggest steam locomotive had 24 wheels. The *Big Boy* hauled freight trains on the Union Pacific in the 1940s. This enormous *articulated* locomotive was nearly 131 feet long.

This is the 1866 steam locomotive, *Peppersass*. It pushed cars up mountains. The wheels and rails were both "toothed" (called *rack and pinion*) so they could grip each other.

I didn't know that

the *Flying Hamburger* was a train. In 1933 this German *diesel-electric* two-unit railcar ran at an average speed of 77 mph – proving just how efficient this type of engine could be.

SEARCH & FIND
Can you find the hamburger?
FIND & SEARCH

FLYING HAMBURGER
Two-unit railcar

Most diesel locomotives are in fact diesel-electric, in which the diesel engine makes the electric power to drive the wheels.

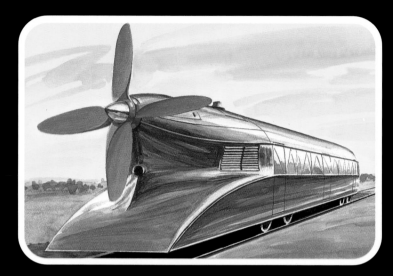

True or false?
Some trains had propellers.

Answer: **True**
A diesel engine powered the propeller at the back of the German *Kruckenburg*. It broke the world record in 1931 with an average speed of 143 mph over 6 miles.

The *Kitson-Still* of 1924 (right) was diesel driven, but the heat from the diesel engine also heated water to produce steam – for that extra push!

Diesel trains began to be used in the U.S. in 1934.

I didn't know that

some trains have several locomotives. Three or four locomotives are often operated by one driver to pull heavy trains. The longest freight train was made up of 16 locomotives and was over several miles long.

SEARCH & FIND & FIND & SEARCH & FIND & SEARCH &

Can you find the four *Centennials?*

UNION

Powerful diesel-electric locomotives (*below*) shunt (push or pull) cars over short distances or in freight yards.

The individual cars of a freight train often go to separate destinations. As they pass through the *classification yard*, their labels are scanned from the control tower. *Computerized points* then send them in the right direction.

DD40AX CENTENNIAL Diesel-electric

I didn't know that

some trains don't make their own power. Some electric trains get their power from overhead wires via a metal *pantograph* on the roof, others from a *conductor rail* on the ground.

SEARCH & FIND
Can you find the steam engine?
& FIND SEARCH

In 1883, Britain's first electric railroad ran along the seafront in Brighton, England.

The *Regio Runners* in Holland (right) are double-decker inter-city trains, powered from overhead electric wires.

 True or false?

There were electric trains more than one hundred years ago.

Answer: **True**

Werner von Siemens (*below*) gave a demonstration of his electric locomotive in Berlin in 1879.

French
CLASS 12000
Electric locomotive

True or false?

Some trains don't need drivers.

Answer: **True**

The Docklands Light Railway (DLR, right) in London, England, and the Bay Area Rapid Transit system (BART) that runs under San Francisco Bay are operated from control centers by computers. A supervisor travels on board the DLR in case anything goes wrong.

SEARCH & FIND & SEARCH & FIND

Can you find four mice?

I didn't know that

trains run beneath the city.

The oldest (1863) and longest underground system is in London. Underground rail systems are now used all over the world.

Thousands of commuters use Japan's Tokyo Underground. Attendants help to shove them onto the busy trains.

London's underground electric "tube" train in England

21

I didn't know that

high-speed trains cruise at 185 mph. The French *TGV* regularly travels at this speed. In 1964, the Japanese *Shinkansen* or *Bullet* train was the first high-speed train. Now the French *TGV* can equal its top speed.

SHINKANSEN SERIES 300
High-speed electric *Bullet* train

 The high-speed *Shinkansen* takes three hours, twelve minutes to travel 320 miles from Osaka to Tokyo. How fast is it going?

Eurostar speeds from London to Paris in three hours. It goes under the English Channel from Folkestone to Calais in only 19 minutes. It is a British design based on the *TGV*.

 True or false?

Some high-speed trains lean over when they go around corners.

Answer: **True**

Trains that lean into curves like a cyclist on a bicycle can go faster around bends. Computers on the Italian *ETR* and the Swedish *X2000* (below) tell the train how far to lean as it goes around the bends.

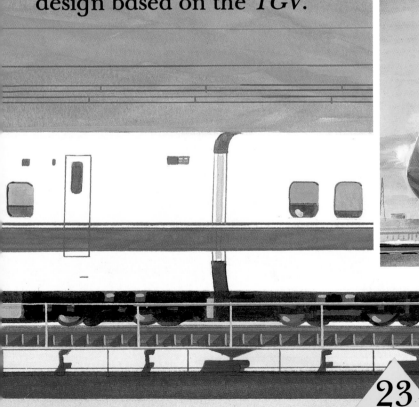

The Ballybunion Line in Ireland was a monorail system from 1888-1924. Invented by a Frenchman, Charles Lartigue, the double engine rode on an A-shaped line.

I didn't know that

some trains run on only one rail. A *monorail* train rides either above or below a single rail. Two vertical wheels guide it along the track and horizontal wheels grip the sides. Sydney's monorail is built on stilts.

A train with no wheels! *TACV* stands for "tracked air cushion vehicle" – a hovercraft on rails. This experimental Aérotrain is powered by a jet plane's engine.

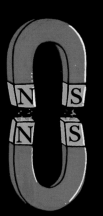

The power of electromagnets can lift a train above the tracks so that it runs without friction, like this *Maglev* train. If you experiment with two ordinary magnets you will discover just how strong their pulls (attraction) and pushes (repulsion) can be.

A *MAGLEV* in Birmingham, England

Sydney, Australia's *AEG von Roll* monorail

I didn't know that

streetcars run on rails in the road. They travel with overhead wires for power. They are popular because they produce less pollution than buses or cars.

Sheffield's Supertram system, England.

11

26

Not all trains look like trains. This railcar, built in 1932 for the County Donegal Joint Railways in Ireland, looks much more like a bus!

 True or false?

The cars on a *cable railroad* have electric engines.

Answer: **False**

The famous cable cars in San Francisco are pulled along by a moving loop of steel cable. The cable runs along a slot in between the rails and the cars clamp onto it.

A diesel railcar in County Donegal, Ireland clocked up nearly one million miles.

I didn't know that some trains run upside down. Rollercoasters run on rails. They are scary but not dangerous. Speed and gravity secure them. Many have hooks around the rails to hold them safely in place.

Have a whole rail network in your own room! Most models are replicas of full-size trains. They are usually electric.

SEARCH & FIND

Can you find the ice cream?

True or false?

Some miniature trains carry passengers.

Answer: **True**

You can visit real miniature railroads and even ride on some of them. This one is steam-powered and is one-fifth the size of the original it has been copied from.

Glossary

Articulated
Built in connected sections. Helps long vehicles to go around bends more easily.

Cable railroad
A railroad where passenger cars are pulled along by a moving cable, operated by a stationary motor.

Computerized
Any system that is controlled by computers.

Classification yard
A place where freight cars are shunted (pushed or pulled) to make up trains.

Conductor rail
Electrified rail that passes electricity to an electric train.

Cylinder
Sealed tube in which gas expands to push a piston.

Diesel-electric
On diesel-electric trains the diesel engine powers a generator that provides electricity for the motor.

Gauge
The distance between the two rails on a railroad track.

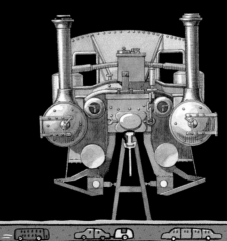

Maglev

Short for "magnetic levitation." A train that is moved along above the track by magnetism.

Monorail

Railcars that run on one rail.

Pantographs

The metal frames on top of an electric train that pick up the electric current from overhead wires.

Piston

The disk that moves inside the cylinder, attached to a rod that turns a crankshaft or flywheel.

Points

A junction where rails can be moved to send a train in a different direction.

Rack and pinion

A system of notched wheels and rails used on mountain railroads.

TACV

Tracked Air Cushion Vehicle – one that moves on a cushion of air above a track.

Wheel combination

The way in which a locomotive's leading (front), driving, and trailing (back) wheels are arranged.

Index

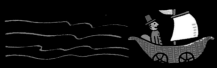